W9-AMB-568

MERMAIDS

DiscoverRoo
An Imprint of Pop!
popbooksonline.com

Martha London

abdobooks.com

Published by Pop!, a division of ABDO, PO Box 398166, Minneapolis, Minnesota 55439. Copyright © 2020 by POP, LLC. International copyrights reserved in all countries. No part of this book may be reproduced in any form without written permission from the publisher. Pop!™ is a trademark and logo of POP, LLC.

Printed in the United States of America, North Mankato, Minnesota.

102019
012020

THIS BOOK CONTAINS RECYCLED MATERIALS

Cover Photo: Shutterstock Images
Interior Photos: Shutterstock Images, 1, 5, 6, 7, 8–9, 11, 16, 19, 20, 21, 22, 23, 25, 26, 27, 28, 28–29, 30; iStockphoto, 12–13, 17 (top), 31; Red Line Editorial, 15; Walt Disney/AF Archive/Alamy, 17 (bottom)

Editor: Sophie Geister-Jones
Series Designer: Jake Nordby

Library of Congress Control Number: 2019942470

Publisher's Cataloging-in-Publication Data

Names: London, Martha, author.

Title: Mermaids / by Martha London

Description: Minneapolis, Minnesota : Pop!, 2020 | Series: Mythical creatures | Includes online resources and index.

Identifiers: ISBN 9781532165795 (lib. bdg.) | ISBN 9781532167119 (ebook)

Subjects: LCSH: Mythical animals--Juvenile literature. | Mermaids--Juvenile literature. | Folklore--Juvenile literature. | Legends--Juvenile literature. | Animals and history--Juvenile literature.

Classification: DDC 398.45--dc23

WELCOME TO DiscoverRoo!

Pop open this book and you'll find QR codes loaded with information, so you can learn even more!

Scan this code* and others like it while you read, or visit the website below to make this book pop!

WITHDRAWN
popbooksonline.com/mermaids

*Scanning QR codes requires a web-enabled smart device with a QR code reader app and a camera.

TABLE OF CONTENTS

CHAPTER 1
SOMETHING IN THE WATER

A sailor stood on the deck of his ship. A soft breeze tickled his face as he watched the water. Suddenly, the sailor heard a splash. A woman was swimming toward the ship.

WATCH A VIDEO HERE!

Many stories say mermaids sit
on rocks and sing to sailors.

Depending on the story, mermaids can be helpful or harmful to sailors.

A tail rose out of the water behind

her. Its green scales glistened in the

sun. She was a mermaid! The sailor

was afraid. He had heard that mermaids

were dangerous.

But this mermaid was kind.
She told the sailor a storm
was coming. The ship
needed to get to safety.
The sailor thanked her
and rushed below deck. He
and his crew steered the ship toward a
shore. Huge waves crashed behind them.
The mermaid's warning saved the sailors.

DID YOU KNOW? Researchers believe sea animals like manatees and dolphins may have inspired stories of mermaids.

People may have
told mermaid stories
after they saw
manatees rise to the
ocean's surface.

CHAPTER 2
MERMAIDS IN HISTORY

Stories of mermaids date back thousands of years. Some of these stories describe merfolk as gods and goddesses. As a result, the mermaids had magical powers.

LEARN MORE HERE!

The earliest description of a mermaid-like figure was the Syrian goddess Atargatis.

They could use these powers to change the weather on the ocean.

For example, stories from ancient Greece describe a merman named Triton. He was the son of the ocean god and goddess. Triton controlled the seas with a shell. He could create a storm or calm the waves.

Images of Triton often have him holding a trident. This weapon looks like a three-pronged fork.

DID YOU KNOW? Oannes was a merman and god from ancient Mesopotamia. **Legends** say Oannes taught people how to read and write.

Many **cultures** have stories about mermaids. These stories come from all over the world. West Africa, Japan, and Northern Europe are just a few examples.

Each culture had a different description of mermaids. Many cultures said mermaids lived in the ocean. But **landlocked** areas told stories of freshwater mermaids. These mermaids lived in rivers and lakes.

WHERE DID MERMAID TALES COME FROM?

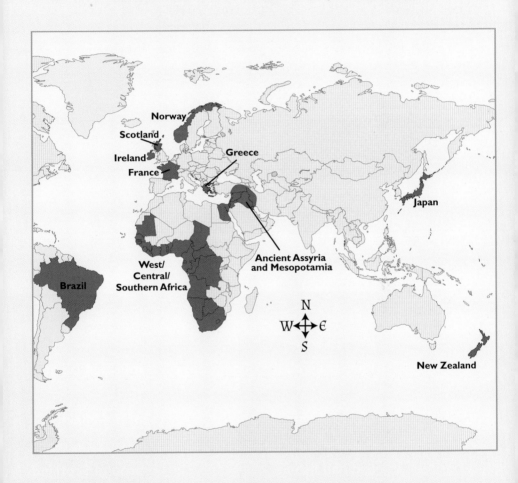

MERMAIDS THROUGH THE YEARS

750 BCE

Greek writer Homer writes stories with mermaids in them.

77 CE

Roman writer Pliny the Elder mentions a creature that is half woman and half fish in his book *Natural History*.

800 CE

Stories of mermen called the Blue Men of the Minch begin to spread around Scotland after several shipwrecks.

1492
Christopher Columbus claims to spot a mermaid when he reaches North America.

2006
Aquamarine is released in theatres. The film features mermaids.

1836
Hans Christian Andersen writes "The Little Mermaid."

CHAPTER 3
FISH OR HUMAN?

Mermaids are half human and half fish.

They have the upper body and face of

a human. Most stories about merfolk

say they have a fish tail. In some stories,

they can shed their tails to walk on land.

COMPLETE AN ACTIVITY HERE!

Some people believe that mermaids live in the sunken city of Atlantis.

Other merfolk must stay in the water.

In fact, some stories tell of mermaids

building underwater cities.

Merfolk are often described as beautiful. Depending on where mermaids live, their skin and clothes can be all different colors. Some stories say mermaids

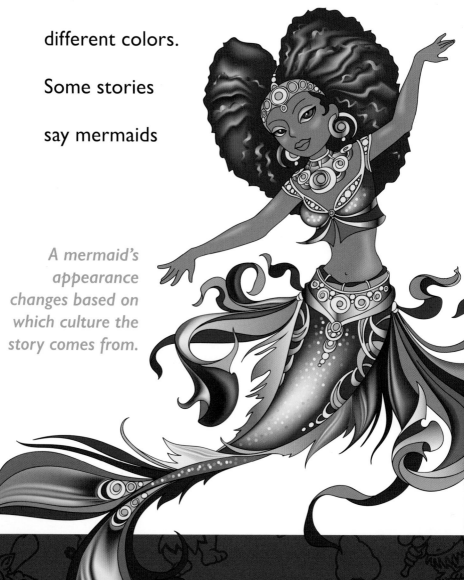

A mermaid's appearance changes based on which culture the story comes from.

must come to the surface to breath. In other stories, they have **gills**. Some **legends** describe mermaids with sharp teeth and spines down their necks and backs.

"The Seal's Skin" is an Icelandic folktale about selkies.

Selkies are similar to mermaids. They are human-like creatures. But they take the shape of seals. Selkies can take off their seal skin and leave the water. They bury their seal skin so no one can find it. If they lose their skin, selkies can never return to the ocean. But with their skin, they can move in and out of the water.

The Hindu god Vishnu sometimes takes the form of a person with a fish tail.

In Greek mythology, many mermaids and mermen were related to gods. As a result, they were thought to be immortal. However, other stories say mermaids die naturally of old age.

DID YOU KNOW? Mami Wata is an African goddess that takes the shape of a mermaid.

CHAPTER 4
SEEING A MERMAID

Many stories about mermaids are warnings. **Legends** say merfolk are dangerous. They sing beautiful songs that can **lure** sailors away from their ships. Then they pull the sailors into the water.

LEARN MORE HERE!

In German stories, mermaids were evil and dangerous.

Scandinavian cultures say it is bad luck to catch a mermaid while fishing.

But mermaids can help humans too.

Some stories describe them as kind.

These mermaids lead sailors to safety.

They can warn them about rocks and storms. They can also cure diseases.

Mermaids take care of sea creatures the same way humans care for land animals.

In other stories, merfolk protect their homes. They keep **pollution** out of oceans and rivers. That way, the water will stay clean.

MAKING CONNECTIONS

TEXT-TO-SELF

Some legends say that mermaids built cities underwater. Have you ever tried to build anything underwater? What was it like?

TEXT-TO-TEXT

Have you read another book about mermaids? What did that book say that is different than this book?

TEXT-TO-WORLD

What are some possible reasons that cultures have different versions of the mermaid myth? Use the information in this book to help you.

GLOSSARY

culture – the ideas, lifestyle, and traditions of a group of people.

gill – a part of an animal's body that helps it breathe underwater.

landlocked – in a location that does not have access to an ocean.

legend – a story passed down over many years.

lure – to trick someone into going somewhere.

pollution – harmful substances that collect in the air, water, or soil.

INDEX

ONLINE RESOURCES
popbooksonline.com

Scan this code* and others like it while you read, or visit the website below to make this book pop!

popbooksonline.com/mermaids

*Scanning QR codes requires a web-enabled smart device with a QR code reader app and a camera.